THE 5 PITFALLS
OF A RELATIONSHIP

.

The 5 Pitfalls of a Relationship

What they haven't told you why your love life stinks

Dr La Grande Mason Jr PhD

XULON PRESS

Xulon Press
2301 Lucien Way #415
Maitland, FL 32751
407.339.4217
www.xulonpress.com

Unless otherwise indicated, Scripture quotations taken from the Holy Bible, New International Version (NIV). Copyright © 1973, 1978, 1984, 2011 by Biblica, Inc.™. Used by permission. All rights reserved.

Paperback ISBN-13: 978-1-66287-995-1
Hard Cover ISBN-13: 978-1-66287-996-8
Ebook ISBN-13: 978-1-66287-997-5

Acknowledgements

This is dedicated to my parents La Grande Sr. and Pearl Mason. The most loving and understanding parents any "spoiled brat", "only child" kid could have. Although they spoiled me, they saw fit to impose corporal punishment when I needed it. They also demonstrated the pinnacle of love, care and affection that would be a lesson for any married couple. My mom influenced my understanding and empathy. My dad taught me to be the consummate gentleman by continuing to open doors and pull back chairs not just for my lady but all ladies in my presence. They both gave me a positive outlook and a love for people from all walks of life.

To the young girls and young ladies, I pursued to demonstrate and practice my early brand of romance and intimacy. And where I experienced heartbreak, disappointments and brief love.

To my academic teachers, professors and other instructors that gave me an education that paralleled with my way of learning and thinking. It would later inspire me for most of my endeavors.

To my cousins (who are more like my siblings), aunts and uncles, close friends (who are like family), my in-laws who allowed me to woo their baby of their family, to accept and love me. My nieces and nephews that call me Uncle. To the kids that are not my biologicals who call me daddy, dad and pops. To my acquaintances, associates and affiliates who were my teammates in our professions. To those bygones on whom I have practiced forgiveness and unrequited cordialness while I didn't seek retribution. To my mentor, the late Judge James N. Reese

(1919-2015) who was to write this book's Forward, but I procrastinated. To my Pastor David Cross who refers to me as his mentor.

To my children (Sonja Lynnette, Tamara, La Grande III, Adrianna, Talia, Carlton) whom I cannot say enough of the pride I have being their dad. My children have grown to be successful academicians, entrepreneurs, community contributors, chefs and creative artists. To my grandchildren (they call me Papa La). To my eldest twin granddaughters who served our country.

Thank you for your service. To my children who had or have married into our family (Omar, Pravina, Reginald) who affectionately call me dad also, I love you and thank God for you being in our family, to continue my legacy.

To my queen, my bride Sonja (Strother) for the many years for having me. For putting up with my shortcomings, my mistakes and my lofty but eventual dreams. Supporting me, forgiving me and believing in me while loving me, nonetheless. But more importantly, being the mother of **ALL My Children**.

PREFACE

This book is based on my own findings. Findings that are from my own, experiences, observations, interpretations, anecdotal research, volunteer contributions and extrapolations from other resources.

The information garnered and conveyed here is not to be a replacement for clinical assistance. Nor is it to present an etched in stone template of human behavior when it comes to intimacy and romanticism. I am merely offering an insightful approach to failed romantic and intimate relationships. Not the WHAT, HOW and WHEN but the **WHY. WHY** your relationships have been unsuccessful. Why your romances are going sour. Thus, **"why your love life stinks".**

Dr. La Grande E. Mason, Jr. PhD

INTRODUCTION

Let it also be known this is not for those that are *already married* and into their committed relationships. This is **not** a **How to Book,** but a **Why Book** for individuals who hadn't been told or are unaware **why** their relationships are not a lasting lovey-dovey romance.

*Why it did not last and why it absolutely stinks, stank or **stunk**!*

I hope that within the content of these writings, you the reader will find humor and seriousness. I'm not invoking pain and anguish; I'm presenting content for the purpose of understanding the need for avoidance as you recognize vulnerabilities in your toxic love life. You just can't fake the funk!

Whether you have experienced heartbreak, unfulfilled or unprecedented love, maybe you still do not know what love is. It makes no difference whether you are male or female or the intended (receiver) or the suitor (deliverer) of your botched love affairs and intimacies. I am confident you can take from this and move forward in your romantic life. This information will help you release the funk from your current or next romance. Do not deny yourself of a loving and fulfilling sweet intimate relationship.

The Five Pitfalls of a Relationship

What They Haven't Told You Why Your Love Life Stinks

VANITY

M erriam-Webster dictionary describes **vanity** as *the inflated and over estimated value of a personality or a person*. It also means valueless and emptiness. You can describe that piece of furniture with the same name in that manner. A vanity is a piece of furniture that can be spotted at bazaars, secondhand stores and seen in a relative's boudoir. It's usually filled with valueless odds and ends, knick knacks, socks, undergarments, unmentionables or whatever. Imagine having a relationship in that same vain. Yep, that type of love is as random as a piece of furniture, seen but without meaningful content inside, I jest.

It was once quoted, "nobody is going to stand up at your funeral and say, you had an expensive couch and great shoes. Don't make your life about stuff!" Nobody is going to eulogize at your funeral about your sexual prowess and your extravagant lifestyle unless they were observers. Not the participants, because they will either be too embarrassed or won't attend. The eulogizers will only give such information to belittle, humor or show the cause of your demise. Don't be vain!!

The **Vanity Pitfall** is the relationship that is of an exterior or soulless nature. There is no emotion, only the convenience of companionship. Perhaps friends with benefits and the perception of the partner at hand is an elaborate or impressive being (piece of meat).

Vanity relationships are deep rooted strictly in being "for show". Most likely for social impression and recognition. Perhaps both parties see the other as eye candy, a good lay or a meal ticket. Its longevity is improbable, often short lived with an abrupt ending. The purpose is empty and full of conceit.

M.E.N.: *materialistic, egotistical, narcissistic*

W.O.M.E.N.: *worldly, ostentatious, materialistic, egotistical, narcissistic*

Materialistic will surely describe *vanity relationships*. How often have we seen cases of couples that just are not conceivably compatible? He is too old; she is too young. She is only after his money. Where did he come from? I heard he has a really good job and drives a nice car. He comes from money. She really snagged a big fish this time. Oh, he must be paying her rent to get her goodies. She said he can really work it. Let us see how long this lasts until the next one comes around. She does not really love him; she is using him like a toothbrush. He does not really love her; he is using her like he does all the rest because she will pay for things he will not. We as observers promptly give fodder to, there are ulterior motives, and the relationship lacks substance and geniality.

Egotism receives lots of attention in clinical journals in the behavioral sciences. Being egotistical and having the air of conceit in a relationship defines hollowness. It causes an alpha personality, *me first* and *it is about me* attitude. Someone is going to posture for control, and someone is going to attempt to outdo another. Being materialistic by buying, spending, instead of investing. Investing in the emotional aspect of a relationship. This is how a vanity rash is spread. But as the demands to be the recipient of the materials grows, the value of the relationship can become burdening and costly to the giver. I cannot say a suitor, because there isn't an intention to suit or woo the heart, only to make an impression of exterior proportions.

Narcissism, it is clinically more habitual. It is offensive and excessive. There is not to be self-centeredness in a relationship. Healthy relationships have commonality, modesty and mutual affection while eradicating selfish absorbance.

My observations have seen a series of ongoing relationship types who fall consistently into this way of courting and consorting. It's not a courtship. It is *serial dating*! Vast in ongoing and countless unfulfilling encounters, void of true intentions leading to commitment or a genuine bond for fidelity. One might call it being heartless.

Worldly behaviors followed by **ostentatiousness** is a vain way to couple with a human being. How incredibly deceitful it is to use someone for their riches and resources, falling in love with **materialistic** aspects. Only **egotism** could dictate such conceit based on appearance and material or monetary resources. Narcissism grossly aims to impress the world and not someone's heart.

Being *worldly* is not a sin as relationships go, but it can become an obtuse and unpredictable area of concern for love and romance. The lure of sophistication is often considered an attraction for a mate. It has the essence of being knowledgeable, wise, mature and savvy. But once it mixes with ostentatiousness or pretentiousness, it morphs into being egotistical. It is no less pompous than people buying books to display but they will never read. I have said it and alluded to it frequently. Vanity relationships are empty and over time become unworthy of being a part of pursuing a love affair. *Futile is the heart un-warmed and pointless is the love incomplete.*

Historically **vanity** has its reputation with celebrities, royalty and the *well to do* begin and end with careless whispers. The *common-folks* who mock the well-to-dos, find themselves in a quandary of careless and empty love. Cultural pre-arranged marriages have been coupling partners without the benefit of building emotions and growth of intimacy through the ages. Such arrangements have brought on infidelity, crimes of passion and wasted love. There will be little chance that such love is often not true. History has shown futility. Crimes occur when one is unable to be released from the loveless relationship after marriage. Some of the best movie plots have immortalized those un-re-leasable love affairs, *until death do we part* is the premise. Can you say Henry VIII?

While reviewing celebrity dating and marriage and outcomes. At one time, society dictated a moral obligation and celebrities were paired as a beard to hide one's true sexual orientation.

Vanity can also be used to cure your loneliness. By influencing someone, buying affection and perpetuating infatuation. When the affluent are matched together it is often for convenience. There may or may not be a commitment, just an affair by proxy. The intentions may or may not be meant for a commitment. Commitment may or may not be allowed let alone expected.

Vanity relationships essentially limit opportunity for commitment. If it lasts longer than 6 to 8 months, it is miraculous. It could possibly and has morphed into one of the other **Pitfalls** by either or both partners. And just as prevalent is that party is probably involved in multiple relationships simultaneously.

Once *vanity* is no longer an attraction and things start to get serious, one of you will do a "Houdini", to avoid commitment, avoid being hurt or the onset of boredom. If relationship fatigue sets in, you will go "MIA" without consequence of remorse or an apology. As relationships become useless, fault and blame are conjured up to end it abruptly. *"Quick is the road out from a meaningless affair"*.

The very essence of no apathy nor empathy, is proof that a relationship was **vain** in origin. It was empty and void of emotions from Jump Street. *It was **just for show**, it was **all about the material things**, *it was **just for the sex***. It was **going nowhere** fast. Eye candy, arm candy, trophy dates, gigolos and cougars all fit the description of those that are in it to floss it.

So, if the fact that *vanity* is the basis of your relationship and maybe only one of you are aware of its emotionless state**,** then it is surely a set-up for a break-up. Pitfalls in a relationship have reputations for causing collateral damage. And those that practice behaviors will repeat them like old episodes of The Twilight Zone.

Wow that really sucks, doesn't it? *Vanity* is just one pitfall and as you read on, not only can it mirror and accompany the other four **Pitfalls**, but it may also start to seem familiar. *But after all, nobody told you about this!*

PITY

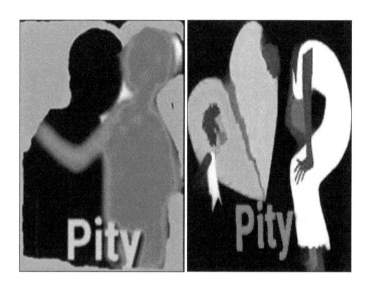

The "feel sorry for" *pitfall* is **Pity**. Such feelings can be acted out by either partner. The *suitor* or the *intended*. Pity is a socially conscious state of empathy or sympathy, to have regret or sorrow for something or someone.

Most dictionaries say (paraphrased) *"pity is the capacity to feel sorrow for one that is unhappy, distressed or unhappy"*. The capacity to feel is certainly a wonderful human attribute. Philanthropic and benevolent sentiment is a positive sign that we can love. Those altruisms cause us to deem one to be in need. Hence, we pity him, her or them. But to present oneself or selves to be in need is the act of seeking **pity**.

Moving forward the subject of **Pity** as a **Pitfall** is presented to illustrate another extreme behavior of failed romance and intimacy. Similar to the **Vanity Pitfall** that demonstrates the severity of having no emotions, Pity goes to the extreme of caring for a partner, by peculiarly deeming them underserved or neglected and using it as an excuse for their faults and poor actions relative to the relationship. Moreover, even trying to dominate them or even allowing them to dominate you.

If the partner is remiss in their role in the relationship, the other lunges into the **Pity Pitfall**, allowing them certain liberties that are rude, crude and unacceptable under normal conditions. They will constantly make excuses for their partner's behavior by protecting and coddling. Even when it is obvious, they are at fault or wrong. Submitting to one's emotional outbreaks as they gain pity. This is manipulation, but when it is allowed its pure **pity**!

It is not unusual for both partners to indulge in *pity*, either simultaneously or intermittently. Both may over-pardon the other for an indiscretion or being curt. And it may or may not be relational, it could be a general occurrence of them violating public decency or social graces.

Here I refer to the *inflictor* or *inflicted*. The *inflictor* feels they can show no mercy because the *inflicted* should know their place and will render forgiveness. The *inflicted* will forgive because they do not want to hurt or lose the other. This type of **pity** can equate to "*getting away with murder*" figuratively.

Not to cast disparagements on people who are in faceless relationships such as pen pals, but they have fallen for the corresponding partner's words of woe and misfortune. They fall in love and make commitments based on their lover's reported predicaments. Sometimes the situations are true, but to be on the side of caution, I would venture to say it is still manipulation. Yes, I'm speaking of prison pen pals and mostly women that fall for those bad boys behind bars. Sending them money or even committing to marriage just for the opportunity of conjugal visits. Falling for the story that creates pity is both naive and desperate. This may sound like something for *Reality TV*, but it exists for real more than imaginable.

Trending now, are on-line dating and distance romances. A multitude of relationships will be challenged as a lack of substantial physical closeness becomes a reality. Often leading to the reality of not experiencing real live intimacy due to a lack of physical presence and minimal connections. I reference this caveat because of the growing number of virtual relationships stemming from social media and on-line dating sites.

I cannot say that there are no real or genuine feelings ever when *pity* is present in a relationship. That would be unfair and obtuse as an objective observer. In the course of successful relationships, the ingredient of *pity* is called **empathy.** Empathy is a real ingredient for understanding. Understanding is a bridge to trust.

Pity can be a precursor to domination and manipulation by either lover. Domination is an old school cultural practice. Domination is who wears the pants, who makes the most money, who controls sexual activity and frequency. Manipulation will have you doing things that you are not readily prepared to do, but you may out of pity be coerced into doing it. All by means of feeling sorry for somebody.

Whoever controls the money (as in today's culture) is in control. And *pity* can somehow cause the sub-dominant or dominated person to reverse control where the dominant lover can be manipulated into serving the less dominant lover.

The mode of manipulation is emotional, and it gains momentum by persuasion of anger, silence, non-returned calls or messages and even sarcasm. It can come as dramatic sadness, crying and even sexual ransom (you ain't getting none). The power of persuasion to get someone to feel sorry for another is manipulation. Especially if it is done on and false pretenses and free of guilt. You will see in the other *Pitfall*, **Entrapment.**

Some mates have fallen into pity, only to mistake it for love, deep like and even bridled respect. Feelings are monsters to the desperate of heart. Feelings have blindly taken over a person's pure intention while it is based on the wrong reasons.

Genuine **pity** is the indulgence of emotional understanding, empathy and sympathy, but it is not regarded as an allowance of wrongdoings and unethical behavior by someone in a love affair. Nor accepting it. Such acceptance is a flaw of <u>overstanding</u> (unnecessary). Allowing unacceptable actions is deplorable and will eventually seep emotional toxins into the relationship. Shit runs downstream and boy it smells so bad you can taste it! *More evidence **why your love life stinks**!*

The existence of these *pitfalls* is not just unhealthy in your relationship, but it's capable of carrying over from relationship to relationship because they've never been removed from your mating DNA. So, when seeking *good love,* and not necessarily *true love* might, if one has never seen what love is. They must be warned about **pity**, the feel sorry for Pitfall.

If I have not mentioned it before,
this writing is to honor love in its purest form.
Love sought to be embraced, to be sustained
*and maintained are the human traits of **need***

THE PARABLE OF ALVIN

Why something Stinks!

When I was a 7- or 8-year-old kid I had a classmate named Alvin. What a nice kid, and boy was he fast. Alvin was the eldest of 5 children. His mother birthed two sets of twins after him. The family migrated to Los Angeles from Arkansas in the late fifties when I met him. Alvin was so interesting. He had a speech impediment to go along with his southern drawl. My class would often laugh at his speech until our teacher informed us his impediment was because of a hearing problem. He had a hearing aid but lost it during the family's move to California and it had drastically affected his speech and his comprehension. I surmise that my availability to impart empathy started early and with Alvin. I understood his shortcomings and I would correct his speech; I would translate what he had difficulty hearing by repeating to him.

Alvin's dad came to L.A. first to find better living conditions for the family. So, once he found employment he sent for the family, and they arrived by Greyhound. They all lived in a small one-bedroom court bungalow not too far from me and the school we attended. Alvin's dad (an army veteran) was really a determined father and husband. He worked 3 jobs with the hopes of moving them to more comfortable accommodations.

Alvin would walk home in the same direction as me but would continue south to his home on the other side of the railroad tracks (yes, we had railroad tracks in central L.A.) The tracks didn't determine a difference of residence, social or financial equality, they were industrial rail tracks placed in that metropolitan part of a diverse Los Angeles.

One day, Alvin decided he wanted to see where I lived. It was a day when we did not have homework for the night. The kids on my block attended different schools than Alvin and me. We would quickly rush our homework and meet outside for some incredibly competitive play of various sports on our street, Touch football, baseball, wiffleball (after a few broken glass windows) track & field competitions and the popular "hide and seek". Being residents of sunny southern California meant we played all through the year without many weather interruptions. Alvin was completely enamored with my neighborhood friends and our activities. They enjoyed him as well, not because he was athletic but because he was so cotton picking fast. Just on that one visit, he vowed to come back,

And boy did Alvin come back! In his haste to come to our block to play (after going home) he would try to run all the way to join us in our chosen game of the day. The distance from his home to get to my block was a tedious journey so he would be too late to be picked on a team. My block was a continuous 4 blocks without other streets intersecting. He would have to cross the railroad tracks, pass by a large Jr.

High school campus, then trek down the very extremely long block. To his chagrin he would be disappointed, frustrated and often sad because we had already chosen teams. Time was of the essence to start playing before dinner time and before darkness would set in. After we did our respective homework, we'd rush outside and immediately chose teams.

Alvin was incredibly determined because he enjoyed our friendship and the comradery. He found a hasty way to get to us quicker.

First it was not doing his homework when he got home but dropping his books and changing his clothes followed by a few chores his mom would ask of him. Then he would head over to 37th Street. Then once he crossed the tracks, he would cut midway of the Jr. High (if the gates were open). Alvin found the backyards of the homes adjacent to one of our backyards to further quicken his trek. Yes, it was a shortcut.

These shortcuts helped him arrive in plenty of time. And by putting off homework, trespassing through the various backs of houses behind ours Alvin would arrive early. Often knocking on a door and intruding on one of us as we finished our homework. Moms are sympathetic when a kid is asking "when is such 'n such going to come out and play?" Alvin over a host of days rang or knocked several doors in search of my home, finding the other kids in the same predicament of finishing homework. He was not familiar with the looks of the houses entering from the rear, so his searches were boldly random.

However, in many homes, most yards had dogs, mostly big dogs. Backyard dwelling pets were protective and territorial and served their master's purpose. Alvin with his great speed would narrowly outrun the dog(s) and then hop on a fence or wall and crawl or leap to the other side, in hopes it was one of the homes of one of us.

Well as it went Alvin brought a real stink with him. On more than several occasions Alvin would be allowed entrance into one of our homes to wait. Upon having a door open Alvin dashed in. His manners had not been instilled for him to ask if he may enter, he just dashed in looking for a familiar face. The first occurrence was a disaster because he ran straight into the Thomas brothers house when he saw them at their table doing homework. Their mom just shook her head and told him he would have to wait until they completed their assignment. But then nature took over, the smell and odors began to permeate Mrs. Thomas' well carpeted living room. The search was short and quick, and the odor tracked right to Alvin. He had a freshly squashed hunk of dog do-do under his shoe.

This event went on through several visits as he would hop fences and climb walls to shorten his journey to play with us. Alvin was not aware of his recurring mess-steps by landing in dog poop. Even worse, bringing it into folk's houses, it made us joke that maybe he was hard of smelling to match being hard of hearing. Cruel humor but truthful without a doubt.

What made this problem even worse, was that when I would see Alvin at school, I would mentally smell poop until I would look down at his shoes to certify there was nothing there. Us kids and our parents could never understand why he did not see where he was stepping, feel what he was stepping in and that he could not smell it. Especially as it occurred so darn often with the same consequences each time. Him bringing along the poop he stepped in.

The point I am making is that many of you that have been in love failed (Pitfall) relationships, have continually brought the same crap along into relationship after relationship.

I am illustrating how if you are dragging your toxic mess from relationship to relationship, all your relationships are going to **STINK**. So, look where you have been, where you're going and recognize where you are. Take a big whiff to be sure you have not dragged some crap along with you. If it stinks, look for it and clean it off. If it still stinks it is where you have been and not necessarily with whom you have been with, but what "you've" been bringing with you.

Human nature is quick to find a blame in others rather than blame in self. It takes more than looking in the mirror. It takes examining your entire being to avoid the bringing of fault, fake and funk (3 F's). I am telling you, nobody has ever told you this, so take heed!

Epilogue of Alvin

The epilogue includes that Alvin would deny the allegations that he brought the stank. He was in such denial at times he would belligerently say, "I don't stank, your house stank"! He finally felt so embarrassed after a while he stopped coming to play. That paired with the fact his mother found out he was skipping homework to go play.

Alvin's dad finally found a steady job outside of L.A that was lucrative enough to give the family a large enough dwelling. His dad took advantage of his VA benefits to purchase a home, but they had to move out to a rural community in San Bernardino County, so he would be closer to his new job. I never saw Alvin again. I can only laugh at the prospect that moving out to such a rural and farming environment (especially in the 1950's), Alvin probably stepped in cow pies and horse apples all the time. We also joked in questioning, "did he ever allow his family to get a dog?" LOL!

DESPERATION

The **Desperation Pitfall** is the "settling" pitfall. Settling for a mate that is less than desirable from the standard how you normally select a partner. When you have allowed underrated selections, choices that are not true to form or allowing lesser suitors, give into that kind of mate and let the relationship progress knowing full well you are not really into it, is desperation.

There are other words that are synonymous with desperation:

Agony
Anxiety
Desolation

Despair
Discomfort
Fear
Gloom
Grief
Melancholy
Misery
Pain
Sorrow
Unhappiness
Concern
Depression
Despondency
Disconsolateness
Distraction
Distress
Torture
Trouble
Unacceptable
Weary
Worry

Eventually you will recognize some of these words in other **Pitfalls**, but for now you will see the quality of a relationship of this magnitude could bring with it the words I've listed above.

These words are not the only descriptions. Nor will they exactly depict what **desperation** brings to one's own relationship. These are words that may have lived and died inside your relationship's past and present. They are here to illustrate just how **desperation** could have been the downfall or *the* Pitfall of your relationships.

I am using "you" in my writing, because if you are reading this, it probably pertains to you. Or that it is so relatable to you (even as a bystander) for another's relationship, it breeds familiarity. Love is not always with a happy ending, but a journey and a page in one's book of living in one's lifetime.

The contents of my writings are inspired by observation of failed and faulty relationships. The result of failed loves I am describing and reporting, I am not prescribing a solution, but painting a words eye view of their pitfalls. A virtual gesturing of *stinking* relationships.

Relationships are a journey into time and space by way of one's vehicle of emotions. That vehicle is fueled by passion and the quest for fulfilment. It is not guided by any form of a GPS system nor is there a road map with lists of destinations.

Human nature takes over like a car out of alignment, pulling either to the extreme left or right. And I have not brought up the component of LOVE! We are going to journey in the direction that brings into view the relationship of lust, lust and lust as a catalyst for desperation.

My findings have seen lust is interchangeable with the word need. "I need somebody", "I need a friend", "I need a companion". "I need to get laid". "I need to be loved". **Desperation** causes *desperate* measures and actions. Or *vice versa*! The cause and or the effect is magnetic, meaning the attraction is based on opposites. I will explain now.

If your preference in a mate is a skinny person but the law of attraction has given you a fat person and you accept it out of the fulfillment of your so-called needs, you have settled. If you would desire a mate that is gainfully employed, but the person that is most available is unemployed and you find out that the person you have been interested in is not willing to be in a committed relationship and is void of being in love nor provides quality time, but you pursue their company, you are **desperate**! If all they want is money and your resources you provide or it's purely lustful sex without reciprocation of any feelings or care for you, that is settling. That is *desperation*. If it is against your moral code, your faith's convictions or your friends and family would not approve if you told them of the arrangements and you still go for their okey-doke, that's pure unadulterated *desperation*.

When you downgrade your standards, preferences for a mate or you are moving in haste in a relationship, that's emotional destitution. The consequences of haste, doubt and disdain with acceptance is a ***desperate*** measure that will probably bring gloom and doom to the relationship. God forbid someone is falling in love. How unfair! But being in relationships that epitomize one of the **Five Pitfalls**, is shallow and bleak (#hopeless).

My dear departed friend PT once confessed that he probably let the "good one" get away, being too picky and too wrapped up in the ***vanity*** of a relationship. He said he was so invested in high profile looking women, he made desperate commitments and all they wanted was the materialistic things he was willing to participate in. This along with some hurt feelings and past unrequited and empty intimacies, he could never trust a lover again. PT died alone.

Loneliness is the mother of ***desperation***. Loneliness is such a treacherous commodity in searching for love and companionship. It is either the magnet of disaster, the forebearer of love in destitution or the offspring of disappointment. It pays dividends in failed relationships with the results in attrition of a romance.

But here it is again. "Desperate times bring desperate measures". This old proverb describes the consequences of doing things that are uncalled for or done with poor judgement out of haste or without conscience. Making decisions that lack narrowing the field of <u>fair play</u>. It is best to allow for mates that are acceptable, of good repute and are contributory to a common and mutual good to be considered. If you take a good look at those you were involved with in the past, you may recognize you were settling for the least and not what was at least decent. In some cases, even mediocre is a better fit. Notwithstanding you could be caught in someone else's ***pitfalls*** of either ***vanity***, ***pity*** or ***desperation.***

When allowing a mate to be in your life and both of you are mutually attracted to one another, it is a far cry from desperation. No one is perfect but if there are any of the following antonyms:

Cheer
Comfort
Contentment
Delight
Ease
Happiness
Health
Joy
Joyfulness
Peace
Pleasure
Relief
Advantage
Calm
Cautiousness
Collectedness
Confidence
Peacefulness
Security

… your relationship has hope and is potentially not headed into a **Pitfall**. However, if you succumb to a lesser quality selection, the intimate and romantic life you have fallen into can be the **Desperate Pitfall**.

Woe to despair, discontent and perhaps even questionable fidelity by either of you. And even you may be a burden to another by being impertinent to caution in your relationship(s).

Strong desires and overzealous passions can also be the "*let in*" for **desperation**. What are strong desires and overzealous passions? *Horny*! Your sex drive takes the wheel and steers you into a pit of no content, no resolve of valueless activities.

Human nature often dictates our emotions. It also may re-direct, upload and involuntarily push you into situations you may not allow yourself to regret. If we do not regret, then we simply are not focusing on what is best. Our sense of need is then cloudy and lacking direction. It becomes want. The condition of want turn needs into base, raw and non-redeeming consequences.

The zest for a hurried life probably appeals to what you THINK will fulfill you. That is the behavior of *desperation*. German WWII General and tank commander, theorist of tank combat Heinz Guderian once said *"There are no desperate situations, there are only desperate people"*. Wherever you are in a state having to do, be or have something in a hurry and you think you need it immediately, but you can only obtain it indiscreetly, immorally or illegally or inconsequentially then you are acting in classic desperation.

American protestant clergyman and academic leader who was noted for his work as an ecumenical American Protestant clergyman and academic leader who was noted for his work in ecumenical relations Douglas Horton is quoted, *"Desperation is like stealing from the Mafia: you stand a good chance of attracting the wrong attention."*

Being in love or pursuing love is a large pill to swallow. It is either medicine to heal or an attempt to self-medicate while taking the wrong type of medicine. Then it hurts trying to get it to go down. Acts of your *desperation* to swallow it will nearly drown you by drinking too much water, then once it gets down, you suffer a scratchy lump in your throat for a bit.

Beginning a love journey without quality appraisals is more desperation than adventure. Love relationships are often influenced by magazines, novels, movies, TV shows or other people. It is not of our own creative choices. Afterall, no one has told you how to find a relationship for love. It is not taught in school, colleges, Sunday school or even in the home. That is why more often than remorse is why your love relations fail!

Desperation paired with despair will plummet you into "this Pitfall". *"Finding permanent and universal cause for misfortune is the practice of despair"*, quoting modern psychologist, Martin Seligman. Award winning singer and songwriter Stephanie Mills once was quoted *"Despair is not a particularly respectable condition and yet despair and delight alternate like systole and diastole in my heart".*

So, if settling for unfulfilled love is pulling at your heartstrings, then perhaps you are operating in **Desperation** and destined to drift into its Pitfall. This is the pit or open hole more like being in a mudslide or quicksand, slowly sifting, sinking and wafting into an unknown bottomless abyss that would be most difficult to escape from. The proverbial slippery slope!

In taking an example from **entrapment**, biological clocks ticking can also be the catalyst or the pull toward **desperation**. Perhaps you are at an *ish age* (30,40,50 ish), seeing family and friends getting married and having babies or are married or in committed relationships with children. So, you're not showing up to special events and family functions without an escort, mate or partner. This causes a rush into a relationship just so you are not the odd one out or *left alone, left behind.*

Can you imagine how debilitating that could be to the partner who finds out they were selected based on a relationship without genuine feelings? A relationship more like bargain bin leftovers rather than a well-planned and nutritious meal!

The ultimate **desperation** occurs when the notion of being at that *ish age*. Your biological clock spinning like a turbofan spinning fast enough to launch a jet. You want to get to have a child before you're too old, or to get married before your parent(s) kick the bucket. This occurs with both men and women in desperation.

Any biological ready and able body will do without the reservation of emotional caring for a willing participant. An ongoing occurrence of **desperation**. But what happens when the feat was without sincerity and the partner or mate is a victim to an empty unparalleled love affair.

The fate of marrying the wrong person was once the punchline of the late comedian Robin Harris, who said that he wore his wedding band on the wrong hand because he married the wrong (explicative) woman. And the American standard pop song says, "fools rush in, where angels fear to tread". That should be the anthem for lovers on the shores of **desperation.**

Looking into the pit of lost or failed love is a painful view. The hurt and despair that was brought on by thoughtless consequences affects all parties involved.

I have seen it affect entire families and their following generations. Not only the lineage, but the generations of children who are the result of and followed the pattern into generational *stinking* messes.

Here are some acts of **desperation** which may include but are not always, nor limited to:

Shotgun weddings
Questionable Online dating
Pen pal dating
Pen pal dating inmates
Mail order brides
Blind dates
Marriage at first sight
Sex on the first date
Sex with a stranger
Pregnancy by a stranger

Desperation is ugly and it *stinks*. The result is toxic. Its toxicity can be mortally wounding and emotionally tormenting. As the pseudo-magnetism brings a malcontent and an oblivious brazened person together, where either or both can add to the toxicity.

Have you ever passed by a public dumpsite? Where all the trash and garbage and waste has come to be buried. The smell is sickening. Environmental studies have revealed that inhabitants of such landfills over time have become ill because of the toxins. Chronic headaches, cancer, and sometimes undetermined or undiagnosable illnesses. Imagine persons dwelling in toxic relationships are often contaminated the same as in emotional relativity. Depression, distrust and worst, chronic ***desperation***. It can be dangerous. But when the unexpecting partner becomes blindly victimized, it is tragic. Unless you're in a desperate state of mind, you don't want to be a substitute or a pawn in someone's anguished love quest. We all strive for a sincere form of love and genuine romance. Not a meal partner in dumpster dive.

Desperation versus *impulses*, triggers different consequences. Impulse relationships usually reason and are probably based on more positive past experiences. ***Desperation*** is throwing all caution to the wind, although it may seem impulsive, it is more calculating and uninhibited to any outcome. Impulse is just to quicken positive merits of success into another level of the relationship. Impulse feeds from the positive and ***desperations*** dives into the known dangers.

ENTRAPMENT

The deceitful **Pitfall**. Conniving and the consequences of luring a mate or loved one so they do not leave the relationship. Like a TV crime show that features the methods to lure the perp back to the scene of the crime or to have them confess to the deed. This method of coercion with false promises is then rewarded with a lighter or full-on sentencing. By any means necessary to get the culprit, perp or even a victim to participate in an illicit activity.

Plotting to keep a lover entangled in a relationship that a lover wants to terminate is **Entrapment**. Holding them hostage, powerless or making things seem hopeless for them to be released from the relationship or affair is entrapment, it should be a crime in the **Court of Love**.

We know in criminal cases it has a gray line and often such evidence is sometimes thrown out or is inadmissible. Such practices are deemed unethical practice.

Certain practices of **entrapment** are often successful enough to hoodwink the targeted love interest. It is so convincing that the intended person never knew that they were marked from the get-go. Wow! If you are asking how someone could be so naive, so blind, so dumb and so stupid well look in the mirror. The power of love is that stealth. So fast that it is undetectable.

Love's furtiveness can be cunning when one allows themself to be vulnerable. Much like **desperation**, taking desperate measures to not let go of a love affair is both unintelligible and selfish. Like a game of poker with marked cards. There lies a disadvantage to one and advantage to another. Gain with the consequence of pain.

The Pitfall of **Entrapment** is a conspiracy and not a natural effort to keep a relationship in decline or termination with a false sincerity. Invoking vulnerability by seduction and promises that have ludicrous intent. All in the spirit of keeping an unwilling lover/ex-lover.

The tactics are absurd and are inclusive of threats of harm in various ways. Sometimes threatening suicide and self-inflictions. Threats of inconvenience, cutting off cell phone privileges and banking usage. Ultimatums of litigation over fiduciary responsibilities like shared rent, leases or other collateral. Even when there are no official matrimonial agreements. But when there are, breaking up becomes complicated. Often the cases in domestic partnerships become just as ugly as divorce although the letter of the law is written differently.

Journalist Flora Rheta Schreiber once said, "The anger. The terror. The feeling of entrapment, the profound distrust of people." Yet some relationships that get pulled into entrapment will fall into the *Stockholm syndrome*, accepting their capturer with a deep affection and unable to let go.

The "big culprit" as an entrapment, is the pregnancy card. Lord have mercy on the morning stars. Paternity and the claim for paternity runs amuck in the archives of the World's courts. Momma's baby, daddy's maybe. Baby Mamma drama. Daddy pays "*cuz*" the DNA.

Daddy's baby, Mamma's payday and so on and so forth. The fact that a woman gets pregnant just to keep a man or a man gets a woman pregnant just so he can keep her. Devastating situations because the child in question is the one that will suffer. That child could be a victim of circumstances the rest of his or her life. Just the fact a child could face rejection, avoidance or even abandonment is sad.

I've been infatuated with the lovely erudite and sagacious TV Judge, **Lauren Lake** on her syndicated show, **Paternity Court**. The show has real life cases of couples resolving the paternity of a child and even adult children coming to prove their relationship to a father that wasn't in their life. I have seen some cases where the paternity in question was for over 40 years. The cases are emotionally taxing, as I watch in intrigue, disgust and anger.

Not too often do I feel the tinge of empathizing with the men and women when the paternity of a child or children is connected to **entrapment** in the relationship. A good portion of the cases also include playing tit for tat, which may be an act found in our next *pitfall*. It's a damn shame when sometimes the child is just the result of some scheme to deceive someone, to snarl them so they won't go. It's appalling when a paternity is charged as the man leaves for another woman. Paternity becomes the focal point primarily because he moved on. Nevertheless, even when he's a deadbeat dad.

Nevertheless, these consequences occur far too often within the Western civilizations. Fatherhood in third world cultures is an honor and the father takes on the responsibility without DNA test. Court cases for forced paying child support are barely enforced because the child is more often than not, is welcomed into a father's life and he readily assumes responsibility. That father probably has other *out of wedlock* offspring.

Both mothers and fathers do tell their potentially sexually active children to beware of pregnancy. They teach how a baby is conceived and how it is born. Daughters are told "don't get pregnant". Sons are also told, "do not get some girl pregnant". We are taught how to protect ourselves as a means for both pregnancies and diseases but never is it that a person may lure you into a trap by getting *knocked up* or getting you *knocked up*.

Paternity and pregnancy are not a subject of this book, but consequences of relationship breakups based on pregnancy are eventual as the days of "*shotgun weddings*" are passe.

Getting back to **entrapment**, pregnancy is a hold card. It's ***desperation*** in action. The problem with pregnancy while taking not only the mate as a hostage but jeopardizing the life of an innocent child. This is a ploy that is selfish with long term consequences. If the father is successful in leaving the relationship, he probably finds it necessary to abandon the child as he has abandoned the relationship with the mother, so he doesn't jeopardize his new budding romance. More so if it is not approved by his new mate because she may not approve or trust the eventual interaction with the ex-lover. Baby mamma drama. He may have left town and will not be able share custody or bond with the children emotional. Perhaps the father is so fed up with the behaviors in the relationship, he wants nothing to do with the child's mother, thus he abandons both out of the need to avoid any further conflicts and ongoing unhappiness.

The other side of entrapment is carried out in fiduciary conditions. The fiduciary situations include:

Shared cell phone accounts
Shared rental and lease property agreements
Shared real estate and holdings
Shared car notes
Cosigned finances

Those items of materialistic value are high stakes in the game of relationship split ups. And where non-legal dissolutions exists. For the purpose of this writing, when it is pitted against a lover in convincing him or her to stay it is a lofty for the individual. The cost of litigation for relationships that are not bound in the traditional legal matrimony or domestic partnerships is usually not equitable. One or the other will end up carrying the brunt of the financial situation until it is handled in a civil court of law. But my observations have witnessed couples attempting to hold the other with threats that are nonconforming to mutual interests.

My private practice has included *assuagement therapy*, helping the individual sever the emotional ties of romance. Assisting an individual in getting out and getting over a love, that they once thought defined their cohabiting existence. Cutting communal ties causes the need to separate and re-establish oneself in many ways emotionally but logistically, but especially financially too. They may need to supplement their income and revenue with a second job and downsizing their current spending lifestyles now that they no longer have the privilege in sharing funds and resources. *Assuagement* (break-up) *therapy* is primarily for individuals who were cohabiting or married but has included individuals not cohabiting but were in long-term relationships.

New cell phone accounts, new credit card (if they can qualify), new residence and critical budgeting so they are able to cover expenses on their own. New ground, new territory in the life of someone that is now on their own. And the repercussions of no longer sharing a life with someone else can be scary. It even means severing family and friendly associations. Going to a new restaurant or club, gym, church or any other social venue. Then there's the pangs of social media's back splash.

I prefaced the previous paragraph about the fear of being alone as daunting. And it brings on unknown grounds that can force holding on to something that is not worth it or unable to be reconciled. The element of fear is what can destroy relationships. Fear is a trustbuster, a mythmaker and a killjoy. Eighty percent of the couples I've counseled, stemmed from loss of trust. Either because of infidelity, lack of quality time, money misappropriations and disappointments and high unachieved expectations. It affects either a man or a woman in any given relationship.

I bet they never told you this in school or college. And not even in church services.

The cause and effect of **entrapment** is relative to behaviors in **desperation**. Afterall, it requires desperate measures to be so deviously alluring. **Entrapment** was not free from poor decision making or bad selections, but it became illicit when you're dubiously snarling a mate to remain in an already doomed romance. Furthermore, you yourself can be trapped in your own web you've weaved. Sadly, the misery affects you both. Deception only breeds lies and kills trust.

The act of trapping a lover is akin to indentured slavery or labor. by binding a lover into staying as if they owe you something. The duplicity state of the affair.

Wow! Imagine having to be trapped in an environment where you can't breathe or being in a situation where you can't even buy yourself out of the predicament. As I have presented this subject with interviewers and audiences, we have coined it as either romantic *hijacking* or *love-napping*. Shackled in bondage of an ill-fated love affair. **Entrapment** is a victimizing behavior. Its intentions are amoral. In due time your victim will find comfort with someone else and thus starts the rejection process in recognition of an unscrupulous affair.

If you have found yourself to be the victim of **entrapment**, you probably began to feel resentment surfacing. You may've stayed for a noble and sympathetic cause but when you have your "come to Jesus moment", you discovered *you've been punked*. Now you are furious and unhappy, and you ponder the universal questions: Why did I get caught up with him/her? Why couldn't I have seen this coming? Why didn't I get out when I had the chance the first time? This is when the emotional toilet has you spiraling down its drain, mingling in your romantic poop! Pee U!!

As we move to the following and final **pitfall**, I will reveal the existence of another ill-fated love fault no one told you about. **Spite!**

SPITE

H ere we are at the final *pitfall*. *The* pitfall *where you fail to yield*. **Spite**! Where warning signs are posted. Posted in yellow, orange and red. Visible and in plain view. Very often there's real life enforcers at the point yelling to you...

Stop! Danger, danger! Halt and turn around. Do not proceed. There's an opening up ahead. If you proceed it could be fatal. The danger is a great abyss on the other side.

The hole is so deep that we will not be able to rescue you. This may be your final warning now!

Well in spite of such warnings, roadblocks, flashing lights, caution signs and even people waving you down pointing to halt, you continue to proceed, as if you are crossing train tracks with the train heading down the tracks but you think you can get around the gates safely.

OMG! If you have not proceeded in such disregard, maybe you have seen it with others.

Some folks are just hard-headed in love. Letting undesirables infiltrate their love lives, holding on to that which is improbable and impossible. Speeding blindly into unknown territories, treading in **known** dangerous waters of romance. Playing with the proverbial fire consciously and caught in blissful apathy of contrite and control.

The most unusual situation I have seen of a **Spite Pitfall** is when a member of the person's family candidly approached the suitor. "You seem like a real nice person, and I'd hate to see you get hurt or involved in the foolishness that has occurred with the other suitors. You need to.......

GET OUT"! Good grief! So low and behold, they continue into the relationship with the zeal of a superhero, coming to save the day and rescue their intended lover from their botched love life and romantic discords. There are some instances in the human gamebook, where only the Good Lord can change people.

"A leopard can't change its spots and a monkey can't drop its tail".

You didn't listen or see all the signs? They lie, they have cheated. They have cheated on others with you, they have cheated on you with others. They are a bag full of it. If you bought them artificial flowers, they would die. It their car get a flat the spare tire is flat too. They are a hot mess and there is nothing no one can do to change him/her.

There are some people that cannot be saved when it comes to love and romance. They are the villains and monsters you know in horror, sci-fi and crime stories. Bad at love. Bad at romances and good at deception. They have got you so buffaloed, you know the difference, but it has gotten so good to you, you remain just for the entertainment. In spite of the seemingly good intentions, it always goes sour. **P-U!**

By virtue of the laws of attraction syndromes, you continue to be involved in these types of relationships. And in spite of the glaring fact, you recognize the funk in the relationship from your previous endeavors in love, you keep going into them. Perhaps you are addicted to drama, disappointment and dissatisfaction. Ya' think? And in spite of changing your intimate scenery, its environment and layouts, you continue to be a part of failure even when you spot it early. As 14th Century grammatist Geoffrey Chaucer quotes, "*Familiarity breeds contempt*". Careless love from a confused mind and failed thoughts brought on by wrongful attractions will never bring you together, no matter what.

Let us take the *train track phenomena*. Speed and size make it dangerous and there is not anything that competes with the size and speed of a train in motion. This is relative to being in a romance that is wrapped in spending on gifts, going out to lavish establishments and it is becoming a financial crisis. The signs are you are out of your league and budget. You have maxed your credit cards and your late on payments. Living the ***fast life*** is all for this lover.

The only thing the lover is about is in your spending on them, showing them a good time and using you and anybody else. Your menial invitations for a simpler date are countered with the suggestion of going to an overpriced bougee cafe. But you keep on pushing for that moment where you are adored and accepted for just the regular things that don't depend on materialism. This type of spite relation is on a ***track, train wreck bound.***

But there are those in a relationship that just won't quit. They are in it to win it! No if ands or buts. They promised love and they continue to take the punishment that it brings. Love unrequited, love unequivocal and love out of control. Again, let me reiterate it is not love in a marital love, but love that has had more ups and downs and go rounds than a Ferris wheel at the county fair. The ultimate "can't let go"!

I have witnessed firsthand where a man pursued a fast life with someone out of his league. He was arrested and did jail time for passing bad checks at those fancy bars and restaurants in Beverly Hills he was frequenting. He did not have the wherewithal to say no or stop perpetrating the role of a big spender. His *spite* factor became criminal and the woman he was trying to impress didn't respond to his call for bail either. She was using him just as hard as he was trying to impress her. It was vanity that was accomplice to *spite* in this scenario.

Often in pursuit of romance, the male's ego will con himself into being persistent. The male ego is a son-of-a-gun (women aren't excluded from egocentrism). Men can be relentless, sometimes bordering on stalking driven by the innate nature of hunting. Women on the other hand in their relentless attempts for their completeness, driven by pride. Both sexes are passionate by nature thus being possessive and territorial.

There is an adage that says, *"a woman is attracted to a man within the first 3 minutes of meeting him"*. If she doesn't accept him, she will dismiss him. Her style of dismissal isn't always tactful. Sometimes it's rude and curt because she just isn't interested. She is not always playing hard to get either. But a potential suitor may not always read into her discontent. With these situations, some men take it as game. Despite his best efforts at any chance to *hook up*, her mind has been made up quickly whether it will be fleeting or fitting just in that short span of time. If a certain man touches her 3 times then, he is to be bound to her. Thus, begets her pursuit of him. And if there is a lesser of an attraction by that man, a **Pitfall** is sure to be involved.

Men on the other hand are less fussy about selecting a woman. It doesn't require a moment's analysis for quality control. It won't be, mostly because without genuine romance his needs are less esoterically intimate and are more physical/sexual. *Any port in a storm, boy-ee!* Is a man's quote when raw needs are at bay. Men are more likely to treat a less desirable woman as in pandemic protocol. "Let's stay in and order". "We can go out another time". And that is a warning sign for a woman, especially if it occurs frequently. The warning is that dude's not that into you. It's also a sign that he's cheap, got another *shorty* or only interested in you for sex. If he borrows money or expects you to fit the bill for your outings, he's a loser/user, if he seems to have a curfew, like he must get up early in the morning and he has to leave before midnight, dude is married or lives with another chick. I am just saying. Keeping it **"100"**.

Men who find the women in their lives are always asking for a handout to pay a bill, buy some nonessential things or is hesitant in sharing your presence with her friends and family she ain't into you either.

Still if this is you and you continue to entertain him/her, you are in *spite* mode. You could be in for a rude awakening of a heartbreak or worse, an STD (too extreme?) even bankruptcy (that's reality). Men who pursue women that are short on quality time and will not give a reasonable excuse for their lack of spending time with you, they're sending signs.

Fact of the matter is that women who either avoid men or who ration their time like pandemic toilet paper are either involved with someone else or just genuinely not interested. If they only show you love after receiving a gift or a favor are also giving you clandestine signs you ain't the one. The sign points that she is just materialistic. To take a phrase from Kanye West, "*I ain't saying 'she a gold digger'*", but her motives are not for a genuine romance or a meaningful relationship. However, if you persist without receiving reciprocal attention you are pursuing in *spite*!

Women are guilty of not reading the signals and go full steam ahead in their pursuit of a spiteful relationship. When a man lays with you it does not always mean he wants to stay with you.

The continuous pursuit of a relationship without receiving an equitable amount of intimacy, respect and returnable emotions needs to be avoided before the *serious catching of feelings* happens. Persistence is

,often considered chivalrous, but unlike the 3-minute female paradox, there should be reasonable amounts of attempts and after that, move on. This goes for men and women.

Let us delve into other scenarios of the **Spite Pitfall**. This segment will include jealousy. What a serious condition in a romance. Jealousy, has started wars, destroyed families and ended platonic relationships. Jealousy is the state of having resentment of a possession or the coveting of someone's possession. Jealousy is an unreasonable desire to have something you do not have.

When it comes to people wanting to possess other people it is a problem. Possessiveness is as critical an issue in relationships as jealousy, yet it is often difficult to decipher the two.

Possessiveness is demanding control of someone and preventing or forbidding someone else from interacting with others. Jealousy is also prevention of allowing one's lover to associate out of discontent. It is the underlying thought that you are not in possession of your lover and afraid of losing them to someone else. This condition is more associated with a lack of self-esteem. A disorder where self-confidence is inadequate. And lack of trust with suspicion your partner is not in love with you. Tragic and unhealthy dynamics in a romance of any type. These are true signs of instability of the individual, relative to an unhealthy mental state. Another sign.

There are scenarios of how someone no longer wants a lover, but they cannot stand to see them with somebody else. By all manner of understanding, it is *possessiveness*. Maybe by feeling this way is because while you think you are over him/her; you justify the idea of keeping or possessing them in case you want them back. Perhaps it is your way to check out others yet slide back into the old lover's life without consequence. Some have said it is a battle of the head and the heart. The head (mind) is a logical instrument that has recognized the ugly in the relationship. The heart is in a dream and fantasy in a fog, harboring the intangible, improbable reasoning that's filled with possessiveness, jealousy, *pity*, *desperation* and *vanity.*

Spite Pitfall, while is failure to yield, it's also the pursuit. If you
have been warned by a person close to or previously involved with that
person but you continue to go forward in the relationship, the relationship is moving towards ***spite***. If you are aware and cognizant of the neg-
atives of your lover but you're still in pursuit, you are teeter-tottering
in ***spite***. Notice the ups and downs of the relationship. Never a dull
moment, never a lengthy period of peace and understanding. Do you
see the same issues looming large and larger with emotional battle scars
and unfinished resolve? Yet you remain in pursuit and the closer you
arrive to be in this despicable and spiteful affair, you do so with all guns
blazing knowing full well a heat-seeking bomb is aimed at your heart.

If you are staying in a relationship knowing very well the relationship is toxic or you competitively staying involved in a relationship so
someone else cannot have them, it is ***spite***. Pursuing someone for the
purpose of "one upping" a rival lover.

Even when they are already in their relationship and are even doing
well, you try to bust it up, that is some evil ***spite***. Going after someone
in a relationship with the intent of destroying their romance is even
more evil.

Spite is reconnecting with an ex-lover for the purpose of revenge
for the previous heartbreaks that you suffered by them. To inflict hurt
in a current relationship to avenge the hurts you're receiving. To accept
the misconduct and mistreatment by your lover and do nothing about
it. And to stay in a relationship that has all the elements of an unsuccessful romance with the unrealistic notion you can change them and
the dynamics of the relationship, all these are pure unadulterated ***spite***.

Spitefulness is an immoral and logistical sin.

When you engage in a relationship where you perpetuate a different
identity, financial means, social status or exaggerated resources, that
is spite. I will venture deeper in the waters to present to you another
spiteful caveat, to start a relationship based on it being platonic, not
sexual and without romance. But soon as you find a crack in the armor

you go for their heart, that is spite by all means because your intentions are clandestine and intentionally dishonest.

You may notice that this ***Pitfall of Spite*** operates on selfishness and malice. It also is relevant to the other four ***Pitfalls*** how it highlights the setbacks of a romantic self-serving relationship.

CONCLUSION

The Five Pitfalls are not the pinnacle, nor the "final say so" when it comes to relationship failures and demises. These are my *personal* findings, found by extrapolating through observable relationship cases theoretically and allegorically.

Many have theorized and further suggested *how-to's* on marriage, romance and love. From Shakespeare, Freud, Dr. Seuss, Mr. Rogers, *Celebrities & TV Show Hosts*, Dr. Ruth and Charlie Brown's Lucy. I am neither condoning nor condemning any of these authors. Essentially, I am not giving you proverbial advice. I'm merely providing a view of what failure looks like by indulging into the given scenarios of relationship disasters. And "*why*" they all terminate sooner or more frequently than most.

The very essence of unsuccess in love can be recognized in the beginning of the romance when persons involved become aware, experienced and intuitive. Otherwise they will be revolving or recirculating failed romances for the better part of their lives.

Failed pursuits and failed romances are the result when lovers consistently fall into **pitfalls** that I have been describing throughout. **Spite** as the *failure to yield pitfall* illustrates how lovers do not take heed when things are abysmal and unequivocally not do-able. **Spite** also dupes oneself into staying in a love affair, perhaps to block anyone else from having an ex-lover. It is not unusual that although you are no longer interested in continuing the affair, you do not want anyone else to be with a former lover. There I've discussed the presence of possessiveness and jealousy. Nonetheless this *pitfall* is critically dysfunctional and can be volatile to one or to the other involved.

Entrapment is intimacy arrested under false pretenses. It is the *deceitful pitfall*. It could also be known as the *hostage taking pitfall*. By purposely plotting and scheming to keep someone who wants out of the relationship, ergo the act of entrapment. Legal threats, pregnancy, enforcing binding agreements, contracts and accounts. Most common is cell phone cancellations and disconnects and the cryptic reminders of how you have been there for them when the chips were down. The dangling of an imaginary carrot with false promises and undervalued gifts. All to get your lover to feel guilty enough to remain rather than *end it split* and *get out* (maybe Jordan Peele can make a parody to his movie based on this concept). Motivating devious thinking to prevent *breakup* is not healthy for any relationship.

Perhaps the healthiest thing in a dysfunctional relationship is to *breakup*.

Human nature has a liking for need. Need is often psycho-physiologically raw and can be shameless. Need is often confused with love because of its vivid emotions. And when needs (wants) are intensely driven to be met, they will bypass provided standards to recognize. When you've compromised your standards, you have settled for less. And that is unadulterated **Desperation, the settle for anything pitfall**. So, if you're seeking intimate companionship, yet you are failing *desperately*, you may begin to ponder gloom, anguish, and dejection or hopelessness to satisfy your need for finding a lover. Thus, leading you to fall deep into a treacherous *pitfall* that is without escape, a contemptuous relationship.

Being in a relationship, specifically a love relationship where the real feeling of love is at question and the feeling and the points of the relationship are hinged on being felt sorry for, is **pity. Pity, the feeling sorry for pitfall,** can be by either the pursuer or the pursued. When you have an overindulgence of empathy for a lover by letting them infringe on moral and legal infraction and stoically letting them get away with things is *pity*. **Pity** creates manipulation and may contribute to the state of unreturned love. Giving love as the other is receiving love without plans of returning love. However more directly, it's not love but *pity*, and pity can absolve hapless behaviors such as defiance, disregard and disrespect by a *using* lover.

Vanity is the pitfall where the relationship is based on the superficial virtues. Dependent on the external virtues of appearance and importance. It is not influenced by heartwarming affections for the intended. It's about materialistic and possessiveness. Not for a lover's affection but for their effects. Love in this relationship is an empty vessel of lust for life and materialism, fueled by one's ego. **Vanity pitfalls** are of the most popular causes of failed relationships of the rich and famous. Predominantly because it is outwardly without true substance. It's usually about sex and the recognition. Ego! Good looks, good sex, a big bank account (at least the perception of such) and mostly those virtues!

If you're not happy with your love life and are ready to cut ties, whether you recognize faults and unhealthy behaviors or whether you're just not happy, maybe it's all of the above. Yet you continue to swim in rivers of foul loves and romances, it may not be the other person, it's you. Yes, it is you, who's bringing a bizarre atmosphere of interpersonal conflict. You constantly bring along the stench of previous pursuits of spoiled loves and relationships. Who wants to be stuck in some **stank** love affair? Or locked in a relationship that is void of happiness and a freedom to be released out of the unhappy romance?

What it all boils down to is whether you know what led you to your failures of love and romance. Did you know why it didn't work out?

Before now, no one's told you what the pitfalls of a relationship are. So now you'll know why your love life stinks!

About the Author

La Grande E. Mason, Jr is an American author, psychologist, life coach and mental health specialist. He is a second generation native of Los Angeles, California (from both parents). His rich experiences in life ranges from internship at a state mental health hospital to working as a special needs teaching assistant and community college counselor. He has also been a musician, stand-up comic, background actor, wine & spirits sales and marketing consultant, youth baseball and basketball coach, deacon, customer service rep, telemarketer, supermarket clerk and he once fixed a *kitchen sink*.

He attributes his ability to empathize with humans in their behaviors and feelings to his parents. His mother was a registered nurse, and his dad was a professional musician. Their qualities helped define his compassion, patience, creativeness and willingness to service others. His attests that his intuition and connecting qualities are God-given.

La Grande used his psychology degree in the commercial field and worked two decades in sales and marketing in the fine wine and spirits industry. He was a collaborator in developing, promoting and distributing some internationally iconic products. His paternal family roots in music and entertainment inspired to him to use his musical talents and formal training to perform as a musician and also a standup comic (aka Skeeter Mason), hence his infusion of humor in more serious academic roles as a lecturer and writer. He's often asked to speak and lecture at schools, colleges, universities, social organizations and churches. He's appeared on local radio and television to render his expertise in marriage, relationships and healthy family values.

As the founder and CEO of a L.A. based non-profit, Helping Angelenos Live Optimistically (HALO 501c3), he was a contributor and consultant to the U.S. Department of Health and Human, Administration for Children and Families' active years from 2003-2016, for healthy marriages, relationships and fatherhood national campaigns.

Dr. Mason received his undergraduate degree in psychology from California State University at Los Angeles ('77), Masters in Marriage and Family Counseling ('06) and a PhD in Psychology from Madison University of Gulfport, Ms. ('07). He has post-grad certifications in Stress Management and Integrative Mental Health Loyola-Marymount University and also a certified Clinical Hypnotherapist (CHt). He's a member of several professional clinical associations. He is the clinical Director of C.F.E.R.M.S., his private practice firm. In addition he's been a Who's Who in both business and marketing and public health.

Dr. Mason has many outside interests. He is an avid sports fan, wine & spirits enthusiast, an eclectic music listener, as well as a classically trained musician, performing and recorded jazz musician.

Dr. Mason is an active man of faith attending The Liberty Church in Gardena, California. As a native of Los Angeles, California, where he resides with his bride (since 1972), Sonja G. (Strother) Mason is a retired educator/administrator with LAUSD for 34 years. They are proud parents of 6 adult children (all colleges graduates) with currently 9 grandchildren.

Dr. Mason remains open for guest appearances and public speaking. Contact information DrLMasonPhD@gmail.com, 866-773-4303 www. DRLMasonPhD.wixsite.com

Printed in the USA
CPSIA information can be obtained
at www.ICGtesting.com
LVHW072227130923
758113LV00017B/278